Inspirations From Me To You

A collection of poetry

Linnette Rene Alston

DEDICATION

This book is dedicated in loving memory of my father Linwood Alston. Thank you for believing in me and encouraging me to believe in myself. I love and miss you!

ACKNOWLEDGEMENTS

I thank God for all the blessings, talents, and patience He has shown me all my life. I thank you God for loving me and helping me to birth my vision. I thank you God for EVERYTHING! To my loving mother Arnita Alston, your love and support means more than you could ever know. Thank you for being my sounding board, my critic, and my friend. Your love and support are what pushes me to move forward. To my brothers Derrick and Kevin Alston, where would I be without you guys. Whenever and whatever I need you both are right there, and I can't begin to express what that means having you both by my side. As I write this, tears fill my eyes because there are no words to tell just how much I love these three people. I thank God for each one of you, I love you! There is nothing like family! To my friends, my sisters, my people who keep me grounded, Sandra Lee, Shawnee Newell, Paula Price, Stephine Richardson, and Dianna Richardson. Thank you for ladies for being my roots, thank you for helping me to continue to grow. To my mentor and friend Debbie Foreman, thank you for holding my hand, kicking my butt, and encouraging me through this process. To everyone who supported me with my book Love From Me To You, thank you for your love and support. Thank you...I love you!

Life's Inspiration

You Inspire Me

You inspire me to give of myself
Unselfishly and straight from the heart
Not to think only of yourself
Your giving spirit sets you apart

You inspire me to stop and feel
Even when my heart says no
You encourage me to let down my shield
And allow my real emotions to show

You inspire me to love
Although sometimes it's not returned
I'll continue with strength from above
The lesson you gave the one I've learned

You've shown and given much
Life is as beautiful as it can be
You add kindness with all you touch
You my dear friend inspire me

Beauty

Beauty is only skin deep
At least that is what I'm told
Quiet honest and yes even meek
Qualities that will never grow old

Beauty found only deep within
Take a moment to look and see
Beauty found beneath my caramel skin
My appearance such a small part of me

Beauty not obvious at first glance
Beauty captivating and very rare
You find yourself in a hypnotic trance
A beauty that is well beyond compare

Beauty as enticing as the sea
Beauty worth more its weight in gold
Beauty so wonderful to behold
Beauty that is found inside of me

People like you

Like a butterfly on a flower's bloom
People come and quickly go
Practically in an instance
They barely have time to say hello

Before the chance to inhale the fragrance
Before you can behold the beauty
People often seem to runaway
Like a butterfly filled with insecurity

Among the millions and millions of people
There are those who are special it's true
The beauty found in our friendship
Is made of special people like you

It is during this time of the year
I have the opportunity to reflect
Just how wonderful you truly are
The love in my heart is hard to neglect

So to my sister and always my friend
I pray for you only the very best
For the best is what I have in you
And for that I am truly blessed

Change

From the innocence of a girl
To the elegant beauty of a woman
Just like the countless things of this world
The one thing that mother nature demands
Change

From the miracle of child birth
To the day of their first step
Out in a cruel world to find self-worth
Love from Mom and Dad always well kept
Change

Like a field planted with seeds
Love and attention will help it grow
Time the blanket that everything needs
The one thing that soon will be no more
Change

From one thing to yet another
Life is funny and sometimes strange
Of all the things in life we plunder
The hardest thing to accept is…Change

Just As I Am

Accept me the good and the bad
All of the things that make me
Please don't take away just add
Encourage me allow me to be free

Don't try to just my behavior
Or give me misguided direction
Please don't try to be my savior
There's no way I'll find perfection

My outlook on life is simple
Nothing complex and nothing fancy
So if in my face you find no dimple
Look beyond the obvious and there find me

Beauty in the eye of the beholder
My style please don't try and change
So if conservative or even bolder
My style is mine don't call it strange

This is me accept it all
Giving my life its own self-exam
Here I stand strong and tall
Accept me totally…just as I am

To My Mother With Love

My friend not just my mother
Is what you are and have been to me
As close to me as any sister
You have been there religiously

You have guided me through ups and downs
You have been my sunshine through the rain
No one could have loved or helped me better
You were there to ease my endless aches and pains

I will never be able to repay my debt
For all that you give is priceless
I can try as they say until the cows come home
And never have your style beauty and finesse

Opportunities are precious and seemingly few
So while I have the time to I just want to say
No mother could be more wonderful and sweet
Yet you become more wonderful with each day

So on this day and every day I pray for this
That God will allow me to have a love so true
A love that will give a loving and happy family
Just like the family who will always love you

Love's Inspiration

Untitled

Like a cactus lingering in the desert sun
Thriving through hot days and cold nights
My love thrives for you as we've only just begun
Marvel not at any reason why
Just know that true love will never die.

The boundaries of my love do not exist
Unconditional best describes the way I love you
Passion infinite beginning with our first kiss
Marvel not at any reason why
Just know that true love will never die.

My diamond in the rough is what I see in you
Brilliant fire that illuminates my darkest of hour
The beauty of love we share shines its way through.
Marvel not at any reason why
Just know that true love will never die.

Change invades life and this we know
Time and its essence comes with that guarantee
No matter what life may bring my love will continue to grow
So marvel not at any reason why
My love for you dear heart will never die.

My Perfect Love

The infinite beauty of a rose
The sun that illuminates from above
In your hands my heart you hold
The completeness of my perfect love

The freshness in a day brand new
The softness found in the breast of a dove
I smile at the thought of you
You bring me brightness my perfect love

You bring me happiness and joy
You are the one I dream of
I'm like a child with a new toy
You are simply wonderful my perfect love

When time is at last no more
When heaven descends from above
You will be the one I adore
My one and only perfect love

What Would It Take

What would it take
To open your eyes
To a woman who could make
An ordinary day into one of surprise

What would it take
To open your mind
To a woman who could make
The cruelest moment seem kind

What would it take
To open your heart
To a woman who could make
Your imagination soar with just a spark

What would it take
To give of yourself
To a woman who could make
You love like no one else

Just a moment of your time
To one who's real never fake
One to add rhythm to your rhyme
That is all it would ever take

When Love Is Gone

The empty hollow in my heart
The countless hours we spend apart
The coldness of the world when I'm alone
This is what I feel when love is gone

Hours spent alone in my room
Hours just spent trying to heal my womb
Hours wanting to just hold someone
Hours like a lifetime when love is gone

Will I have the chance to make it right
Will I make it through another night
Will there ever be the words of another love song
Will time be my friend when love is gone

Maybe I'll win your heart again
Maybe we can both make a mend
Maybe you'll be the only one
Maybe…who knows when love is gone

In Your Arms

In your arms is where I want to be
In your arms is where I find myself
In your arms is where I find peace
In your arms is where I know love is felt

Shelter from the rain and cold is what I need
A tranquil place that will allow me to be free
A place of sanctuary where my spirit can feed
In your strong arms is where I want to be

Looking eagerly for the meaning in my life
Looking in that solemn place beyond my cleft
Beyond the place where pain coexist with strife
In your loving arms I find strength to love self

Searching for a place where the sky is a graceful blue
For that place where smiles are abundant and never cease
Searching for that calming comfort that's exciting and new
In your adoring arms is where I find my peace

In your arms is where I want to be
In your arms is where I find myself
In your arms is where I find peace
In your arms is where I know love is felt

Can I

Can I read your mind
View each and every part
I'm on love's journey to find
All keys that will open your heart

Can I view the world through your eyes
To see the beauty that you behold
Visualizing the magic in truth
Honesty the intricate framework that molds

Can I feel your emotion
To be engulfed by waves of passion
Spellbound by your manly essence
My heart a casualty to love's fatal attraction

Can I penetrate your guarded heart
Can I erase the intense hurt and pain
Allow me to bypass your troubled chambers
Allow my love to bring sunshine after the rain

I can ask twenty questions
Hoping to take my time
Please know I'll use discretion
If only I could read your mind.

Your Love

Nurturing like the love of a mother for her child
Soft spoken encouraging honest and always mild
Prayers answered from the Man above
The day He blessed me with your love

Strength the calm force from within
Protective yet gentle the thing to help my heart mend
Prayers answered from the Man above
The day He blessed me with your love

Intoxicating like the finest of wines
Inviting enticing wonderful your love is all mine
Prayers answered from the Man above
The day He blessed me with your love

My life's journey now awaits
With lots of love and some mistakes
But patience and love will heal all heartaches
Prayers answered from the Man above
The day He blessed me with your love

Heavenly Inspiration

A Divine Love

Peace to quiet our storms
Contentment blankets us with warmth
One of many gifts from above
The tranquility of a divine love

Joy given to make days bright
Angels all around even through night
One of many gifts from above
The happiness of a divine love

Love washed away my sin
Renewed the right spirit deep within
One of many gifts from above
The miracle of a divine love

Jesus paid the price you see
He died on the cross for you and me
One of many gifts from above
The ultimate of a divine love

Untitled

Confusion enters my mind
As I wrestle with the thoughts of love
Will I ever know what it is
Does true happiness come from above

My thoughts they echo
Like sounds through space
Is there truly someone for me
Will beauty ever behold grace

As I sit in a room alone
To watch the children play
My heart it yearns for the peace
Found in an awesome spring day

When day gives way to night
And my soul seeks its rest
I will continue to look above and pray
I will continue to trust God for He knows best

The Woman Living for Christ

Humility best describes a woman
Who serves with a faithful heart
A woman who surrenders all to God
In God's kingdom she strives to be apart
Loving God with all her might
Humble is the woman living for Christ

Peace sustains her through all her trials
For in her trials she knows God cares
Trusting in His divine promise
Trusting in the power of prayer
Continuing to love God with all her might
Faithful is the woman living for Christ

Wisdom she gains from day to day
Leaning and standing on God's Holy Word
Spreading and teaching the gospel of Christ
Giving no thought to gossip she's heard
Loving God with all her might
Temperance describes the woman living for Christ

Washed is she with the blood of Jesus
For Jesus made a change within
Filled with such an awesome power
No longer bound in this world of sin
Loving God with all her might
Holy Ghost filled is the woman living for Christ

Love lifted me from the miry clay
Instilled in me is a song brand new
Here today I pledge my life
To serve Jesus my Savior only you
I'll love and serve with all my might
I am a woman living for Christ

Perfect Peace

Radiant is the smile that we came to love
And now that smile will shine from above
In God's love our pain will soon cease
In God's love you've found perfect peace

Echoes of your loving voice will continue to last
As we remember tender moments of the past
In God's love our pain will soon cease
In God's love you've found perfect peace

Your kind spirit you always shared
And we thank God that you cared
In God's love our pain will soon cease
In God's love you've found perfect peace

Life handed you some heartaches and pains
And we never once heard you complain
In God's love our pain will soon cease
In God's love you've found perfect peace

Your love was felt like rain from above
Yet nothing compares to God's abiding love
In God's love our pain will soon cease
In God's love you've found perfect peace

Thank you

With a radiant smile and sometimes a heavy heart
I realize in God's service I want to be apart
Through some laughter and so many tears
I thank you God for all my years

At times it seems friends are few
With faith God you brought me through
You give me courage to replace my fears
And I want to thank you God for all my years

I've been talked about and criticized
Yet your love wiped tears from my eyes
With an aching heart and thousands of tears
I continue to thank you God for all my years

I am a soldier ready for the fight
Singing God's praises with all my might
Protect me Heavenly Father from Satan's spears
And I will forever thank you God for all my years

About the Author

Born in Washington, DC, raised in a small town in Littleton, North Carolina and now residing in Rocky Mount, North Carolina is where you will find Linnette R. Alston. A young woman who learned the meaning of love from her own front door. The oldest and the only girl of three, learned what true love is all about from her parents. Being taught how to love and respect others, she was also taught that she had a voice. A voice that should be heard when she found her passion. Linnette's passion…. her writing. Not only an up-coming author, Linnette is the CEO/Owner of All For You Travel and works as a Medical Billing Specialist for a non-profit medical organization in North Carolina.

Linnette completed her first book of poetry Love From Me To You in July 2017. Linnette is also working on a self-motivation book as well as a novel that she hopes to complete by end of the year.